Word 365
Tables

EASY WORD 365 ESSENTIALS - BOOK 4

M.L. HUMPHREY

Copyright © 2023 M.L. Humphrey

All Rights Reserved.

ISBN: 978-1-63744-103-9

SELECT TITLES BY M.L. HUMPHREY

WORD 365 ESSENTIALS
Word 365 for Beginners
Intermediate Word 365

EASY WORD 365 ESSENTIALS
Text Formatting
Page Formatting
Lists
Tables
Styles and Breaks
Track Changes

See mlhumphrey.com for more Microsoft Office titles

CONTENTS

INTRODUCTION	1
TABLES	3
APPENDIX A: BASIC TERMINOLOGY RECAP	19
ABOUT THE AUTHOR	21

Introduction

This book is part of the *Easy Word 365 Essentials* series of titles. These are targeted titles that are excerpted from the main *Word 365 Essentials* series and are focused on one specific topic.

If you want a more general introduction to Word, then you should check out the *Word 365 Essentials* titles instead. In this case, *Intermediate Word 365* which covers not only tables but track changes, multilevel lists, styles, breaks, and more.

But if all you want to learn is how to create and format tables in Word, then this is the book for you.

Tables

When I was in a corporate job we used tables all the time, so this is one that's definitely worth mastering. But if you really want to be good with tables you not only need to be able to insert them into a document, you need to format them properly, too, so this is going to be a long chapter.

Insert

To insert a table, go to the Insert tab and click on the dropdown for Table in the Tables section:

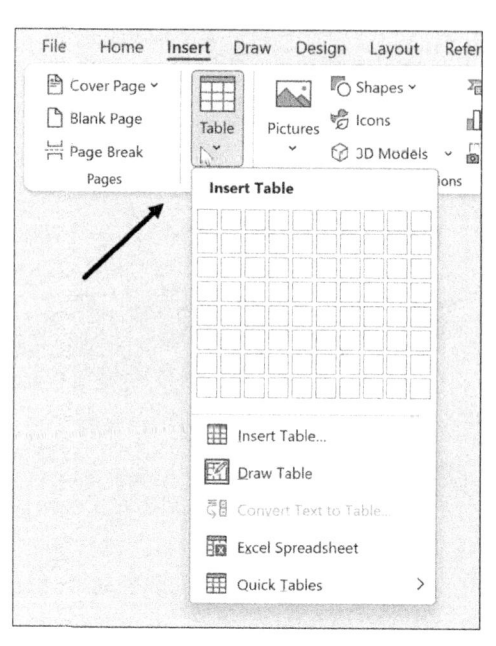

Under that Insert Table section, you can hold your mouse over the number of rows and columns you want in your table and Word will draw that for you in the document. Like so:

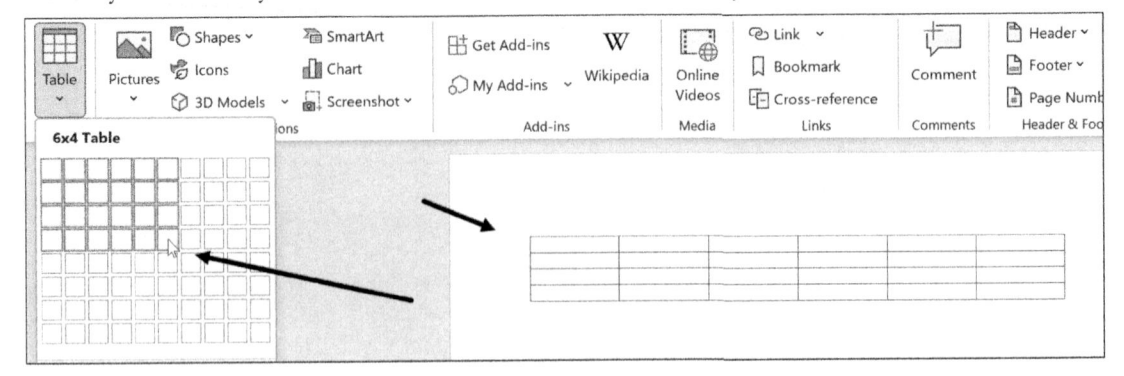

Click to insert the table.

Don't worry so much about the number of rows, but it is nice to start with the proper number of columns. (To add new rows to a table you can just go to the last cell in the table and use the Tab key and Word will add another row, so especially if you're directly entering the values in the table, the number of rows is easy to fix as needed.)

If you click on Insert Table in that dropdown instead, it will open the Insert Table dialogue box which lets you specify a number for columns and rows and also specify the AutoFit behavior for the table (fixed width, fit to contents, fit to window).

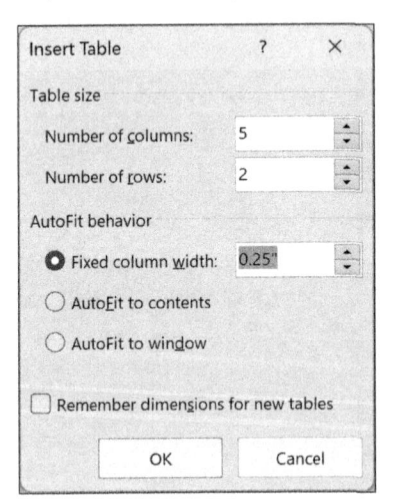

Another option is the Draw Table option, which is located in that same dropdown menu. It basically lets you left-click and drag to place a rectangle and then left-click and drag to draw lines within it, but I never use that option myself.

The Quick Tables option is another one I don't use. It inserts a pre-formatted table template.

The Excel Spreadsheet option will embed a working Excel spreadsheet into your document that displays as a table. When you're working in that one, your interface up top will actually be the Excel interface. But when you click away it will look like an ordinary table. Double-click on the table to get back into the Excel interface.

For working with calculations, the Excel Spreadsheet option is probably a better choice than trying to work directly in Word, but all of your formatting of that table will have to happen in the Excel interface, because once you close the interface Word will treat the table as a picture that can't be formatted or edited.

For this book we're just going to stick to a basic table.

When you insert a normal table in Word, you will see two new tabs appear at the top of the workspace, Table Design and Layout. There are a number of formatting choices you can make there, but first I just want to talk about a basic table using the Home tab options.

Here I've inserted a table in my document:

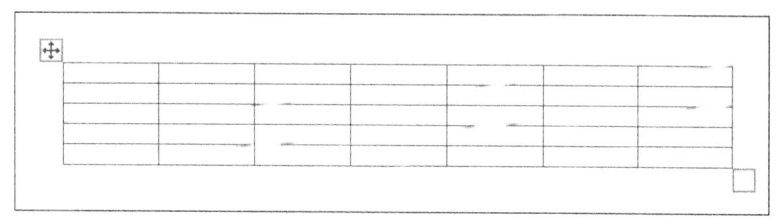

Now let's walk through how to add text and format that table.

Add Text

To input text into the table, you can click into a cell and type. Use the Tab key to move to the next cell in a row or Shift + Tab to move back one cell. If you're at the end of a row, it will move you to the next cell on the row below or above, depending on which direction you were moving.

If you have data to paste into your table, select all of the cells in the table first that will contain that data and then paste (Ctrl + V or one of the paste special options). If you don't select cells first, the data will all paste into that one cell where your cursor was. If you select less than the required number of cells, only the data for those cells will paste in. If you select too many cells, the data will paste in more than once to fill the selected number of cells.

Delete Text

To delete the text in a specific cell, select that text and then use the Backspace or Delete key. If you need to delete text in more than one cell at a time, use the Delete key.

If you select text in more than one cell or select an entire cell and try to use the Backspace key, Excel will want to also delete the cell not just the text. You'll see a Delete Cells dialogue box appear. You can close that box if that wasn't your intent, or choose one of the listed options if that was what you wanted to do.

Delete Contents of Table

To delete the contents of the entire table, click on the white box with four arrows in the top left corner of the table and then use the Delete key.

Delete Table

To delete the entire table, click on the white box with four arrows in the top left corner of the table and then use the Backspace key.

You can also use Cut once the table is selected or go to the Rows & Columns section of the table Layout tab, use the Delete dropdown menu, and choose Delete Table.

Format Text

You can format any text in a table just like you would other text. Select the cell(s) you want to format and then use the Font section of the Home tab or Ctrl shortcuts to apply your formatting. There are also alignment and text direction options in the Alignment section of the Layout tab.

Shading

One type of formatting that we didn't discuss in *Word 365 for Beginners* is Shading. That's because I usually only use it for tables. I like to have the first row of a table use a shaded background behind my text. Like so:

Value	Decimal Places	ROUND	ROUNDUP	ROUNDDOWN
3.124	2	3.12	3.13	3.12
3.126	2	3.13	3.13	3.12
-3.1246	2	-3.12	-3.13	-3.12
-3.1262	2	-3.13	-3.13	-3.12

That lets me distinguish my labels from my data.

To apply shading, select those cell(s), and then go to the Paragraph section of the Home tab. The Shading option is in the bottom row on the right-hand side. It looks like a paint bucket tilted to the right.

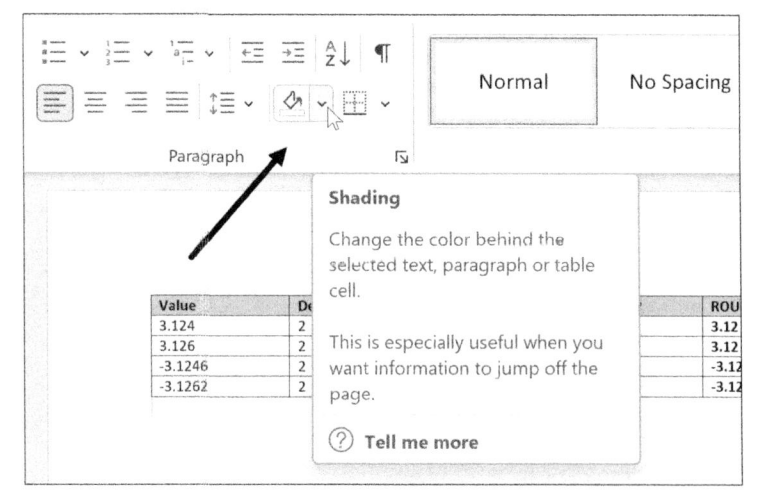

Click on the dropdown arrow to see the available color choices:

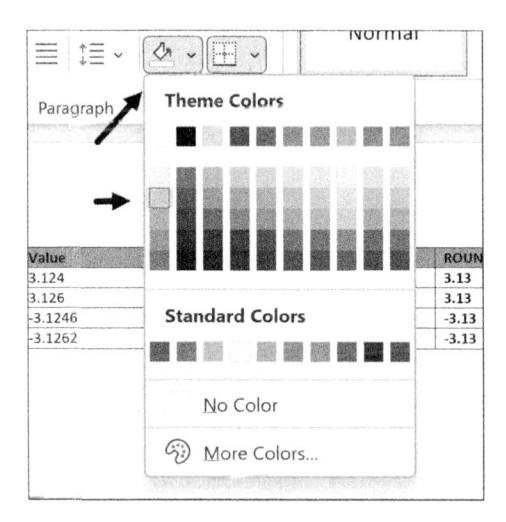

There are seventy colors there to choose from, but if you need a different color you can click on More Colors to open the Color dialogue box. The No Color option is what to use to remove shading from your selected cell(s).

There is also a Shading option in the Table Styles section of the Table Design tab as well as in the mini formatting menu.

Borders

By default, when you insert a table in Word it will have a border around all four sides of each cell. If you want to remove or edit the style of one of those borders, you can use the Borders dropdown in the Paragraph section of the Home tab:

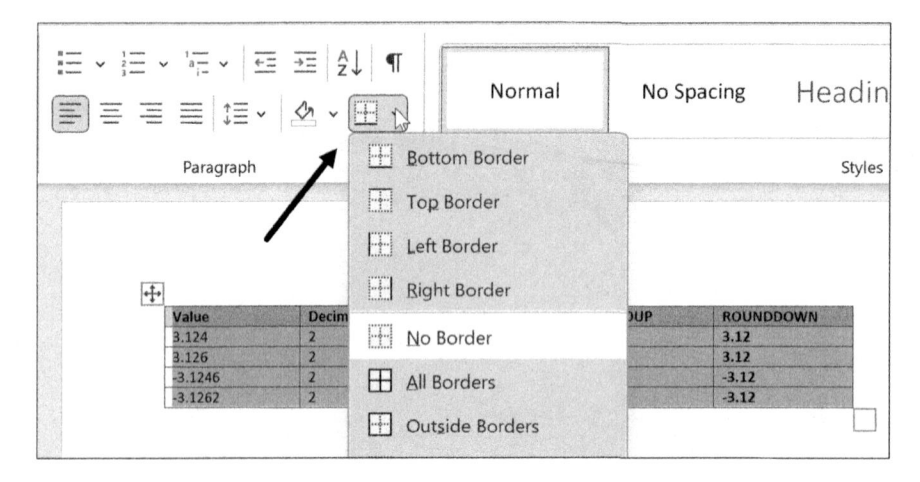

The borders that are currently applied to the table will be shaded in gray. The borders that are not currently in use will be unshaded. Hold your mouse over each option to see what the table will look like if that border is removed or added. Click to apply that change.

If you click on the Borders and Shading option at the bottom of the dropdown menu, that will open the Borders and Shading dialogue box which will let you change the line width, style, or color. Make those changes before applying new borders to your table.

Choose the Custom setting and use the Preview section to choose which lines to change if you want to use more than one line style, width, or color in your table at a time.

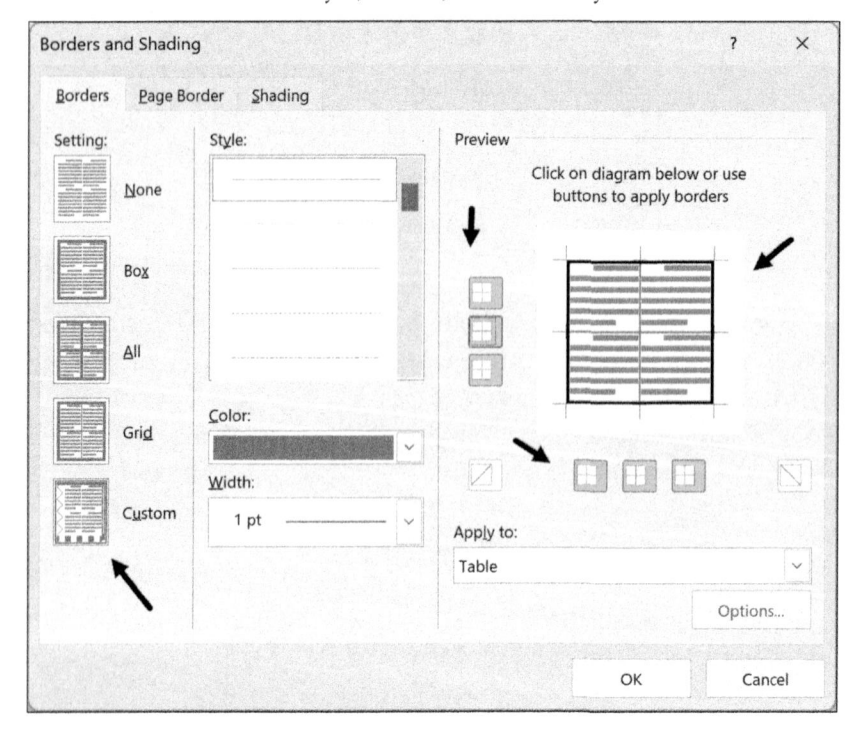

You can also select just a subset of the cells in the table to format those differently if needed, like I did here for the top row of this table which needed a different cell border than the main cells in the table:

Value	Decimal Places	ROUND	ROUNDUP	ROUNDDOWN
3.124	2	3.12	3.13	3.12
3.126	2	3.13	3.13	3.12
-3.1246	2	-3.12	-3.13	-3.12
-3.1262	2	-3.13	-3.13	-3.12

The Table Design tab also has a Borders section where you can choose your line style, line weight, and line color. If you make all of your selections there, you can then use the Border Painter and click on individual lines within your table to change their formatting:

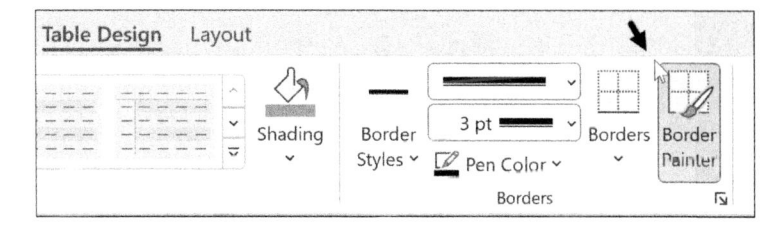

There is also a Borders dropdown menu there, but if you want to use it be sure to select the whole table or the cells you want to format first before making your selection.

You can also right-click on your table and choose Border Styles from the dropdown menu there to choose from a selection of twenty-one line styles which you can then apply one cell border at a time by clicking on the cell border.

Column Width

To manually adjust the width of a column in a table, left-click on the right-hand or left-hand border for that column and then hold that left-click and drag:

Value	Decimal Places	ROUND
3.124	2	3.12
3.126	2	3.13
-3.1246	2	-3.12
-3.1262	2	-3.13

(If you have your cursor positioned in the right spot it will turn into two vertical lines with arrows pointing in either direction.)

If you click and drag in the direction of another column, it will also change the width of the neighboring column so that the total width of the two columns combined remains the same. If you click and drag from the outer perimeter of the first or last column in the table, it will change the overall width of the table.

You can also right-click and choose to Distribute Columns Evenly or you can click on Distribute Columns in the Cell Size section of the Layout tab if you want all of your columns to be the same width.

Another option is to right-click on the column and choose Table Properties from the dropdown menu. Go to the Column tab and choose a new value for the Preferred Width of that column.

Or you can go to the table Layout tab and change the value for Width under Cell Size.

Both of those last two options will change the overall width of the table as well.

I will often combine the left-click and drag option on the first or last column to change the overall width of the table and then use that Distribute Columns option to fix the width of the columns based on the new table width.

Row Height

As you type text into a cell in Word the height of that row will automatically adjust so that all of the text is visible. (See image below for an example.) It is not possible to change a row height to hide any text in that row.

But you can left-click and drag along the upper or lower border of a cell to change the row height so that there's more space than the text takes up. (The cursor will look like two parallel lines with arrows pointing up and down when you have it positioned correctly.)

Value and then a lot of text to give this a new height	Decimal Places	ROUND	ROUNDUP	ROUNDDOWN
3.124	2	3.12	3.13	3.12
3.126	2	3.13	3.13	3.12
-3.1246	2	-3.12	-3.13	-3.12
-3.1262	2	-3.13	-3.13	-3.12

You can also open the Table Properties dialogue box or change the Height value in the Cell Size section of the table Layout tab.

If you choose Distribute Rows in the table Layout tab or Distribute Rows Evenly by right-clicking, that will resize your rows so that they are all the same size based upon the cell that is the tallest. Like here where all rows are now the height of the header row:

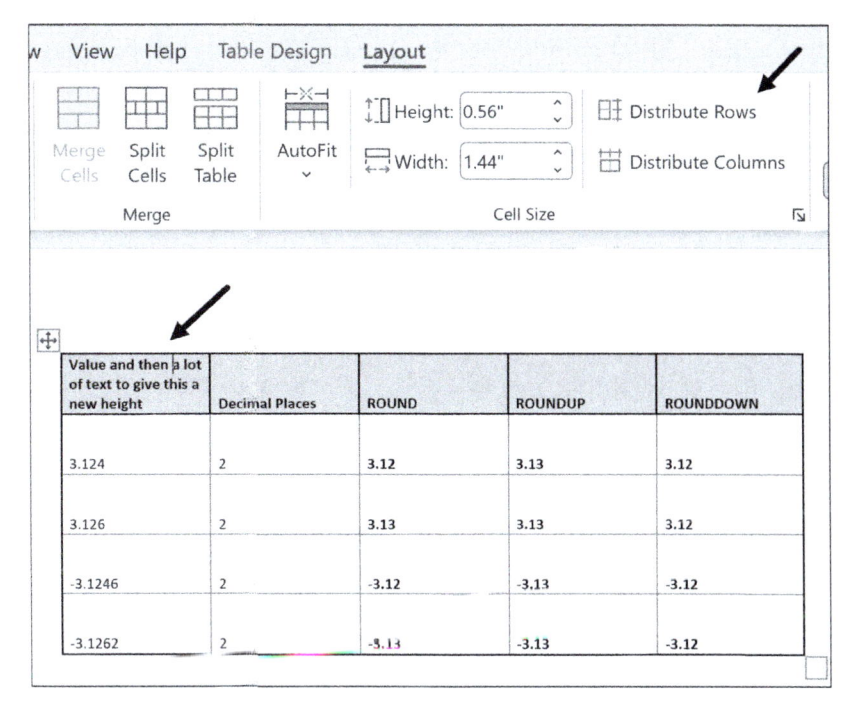

Space Between Cells or Around Table

To add space between cells or around the perimeter of your table, use the Cell Margins option in the Alignment section of the Layout tab to open the Table Options dialogue box.

Changing the value for Default Cell Spacing will add a space between the cells in each row and column. You can see that in the image below where each cell of the table is separated from the other cells in the table:

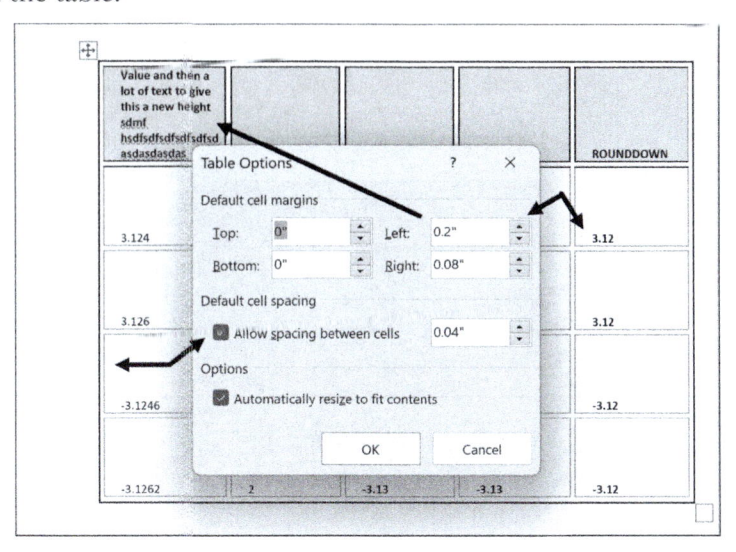

Adjusting the Default Cell Margins values adds space between the borders of each cell and the text within the cells.

You can see an example of this in the left-hand cell in the column header row where the text is indented from the left-hand side by .2" and from the right-hand side by only .08". Note how the text in that cell is visibly closer to the right-hand side of the cell.

Repeat Header Row

If you have a table that stretches across more than one page, then you will likely want to have the header row for that table on both pages. Rather than try to manually do that, which you should not do, there is an option that allows you to repeat the header row.

This is available in the Data section of the table Layout tab. Click on the option there.

Or you can right-click and choose Table Properties to open the Table Properties dialogue box and then go to the Row tab and check the box there.

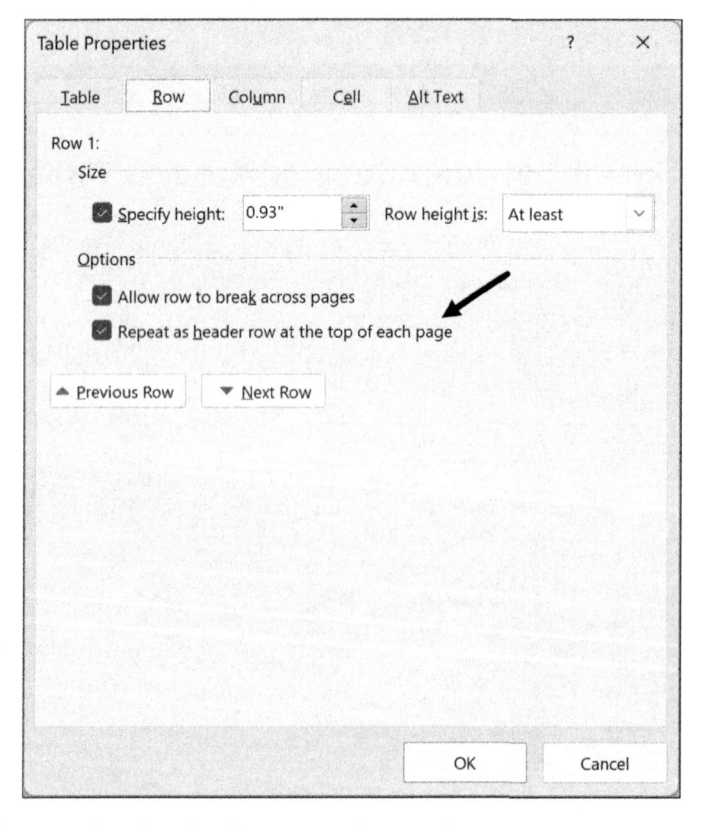

That option is only available for the first row of the table.

Insert Rows or Columns

We already discussed how to add an extra row to the end of a table. Just use Tab from the last cell in the table and Word will automatically add another row. But sometimes you will want to add a row(s) or column(s) in the midst of a table. Click on that location and then you have two options.

The first option is the Rows & Columns section of the table Layout tab:

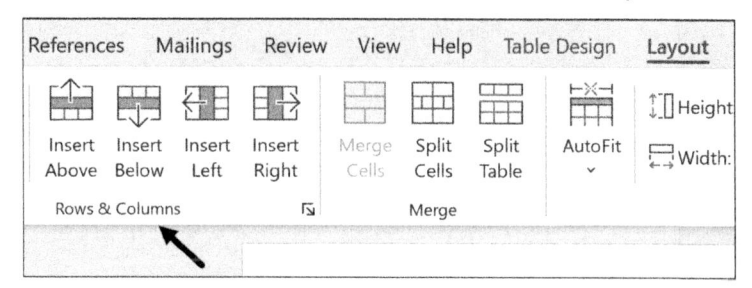

But I usually just right-click on the table and choose Insert from the dropdown menu and then my desired option from that secondary dropdown menu:

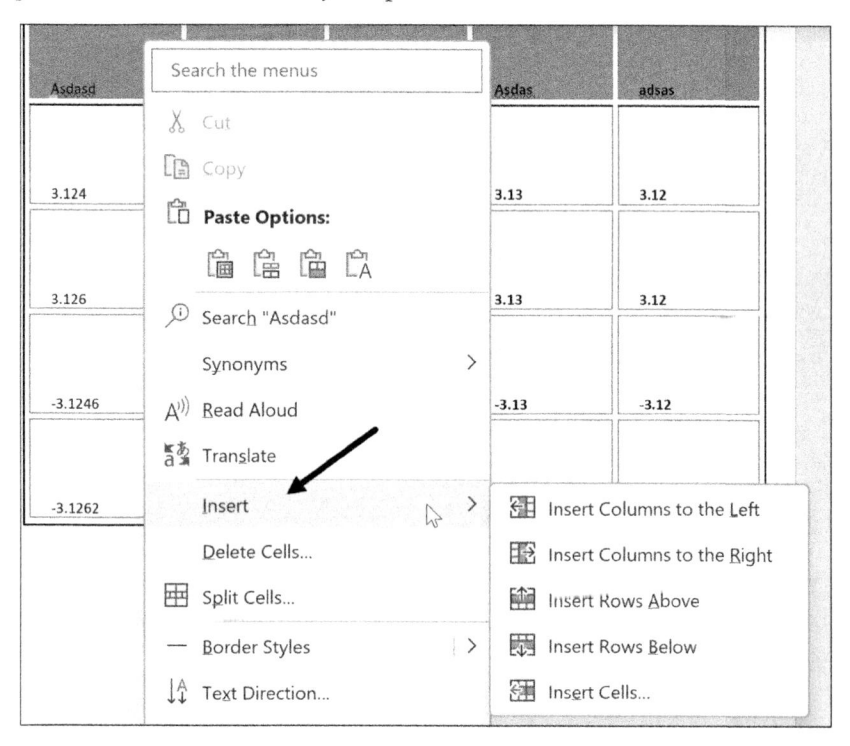

Note that if you insert columns that will change the overall width of your table so you may have to make adjustments after doing so to get the table to fit on the page again.

Delete Rows or Columns

To delete a column or row in a table, right-click on a cell in the column or row you want to delete and then choose the Delete option from the dropdown menu. This will bring up the Delete Cells dialogue box where you can choose to delete the entire row or column.

Your other option is to use the Delete dropdown menu in the Rows & Columns section of the Layout tab. Or to select one or more cells in that row or column and then use the Backspace key to bring up the Delete Cells dialogue box.

Delete Cell(s)

I don't recommend doing this, but it is possible to delete a single cell in a table using the above options.

Resize Table

To resize a table, right-click, choose Table Properties from the dropdown menu, and then go to the Table tab of the Table Properties dialogue box and change the value for Preferred Width. Click on OK. This will change your column widths, so you will probably have to adjust those afterward.

(The other option, mentioned above, is to resize a column at one end or the other of your table.)

Move Table

To move a table, left-click on the square with four arrows in the top left corner of the table and then drag.

Split Table

To split your table into two separate tables, click into the row that you want to be the first row in the second table and then go to the Merge section of the table Layout tab and click on Split Table.

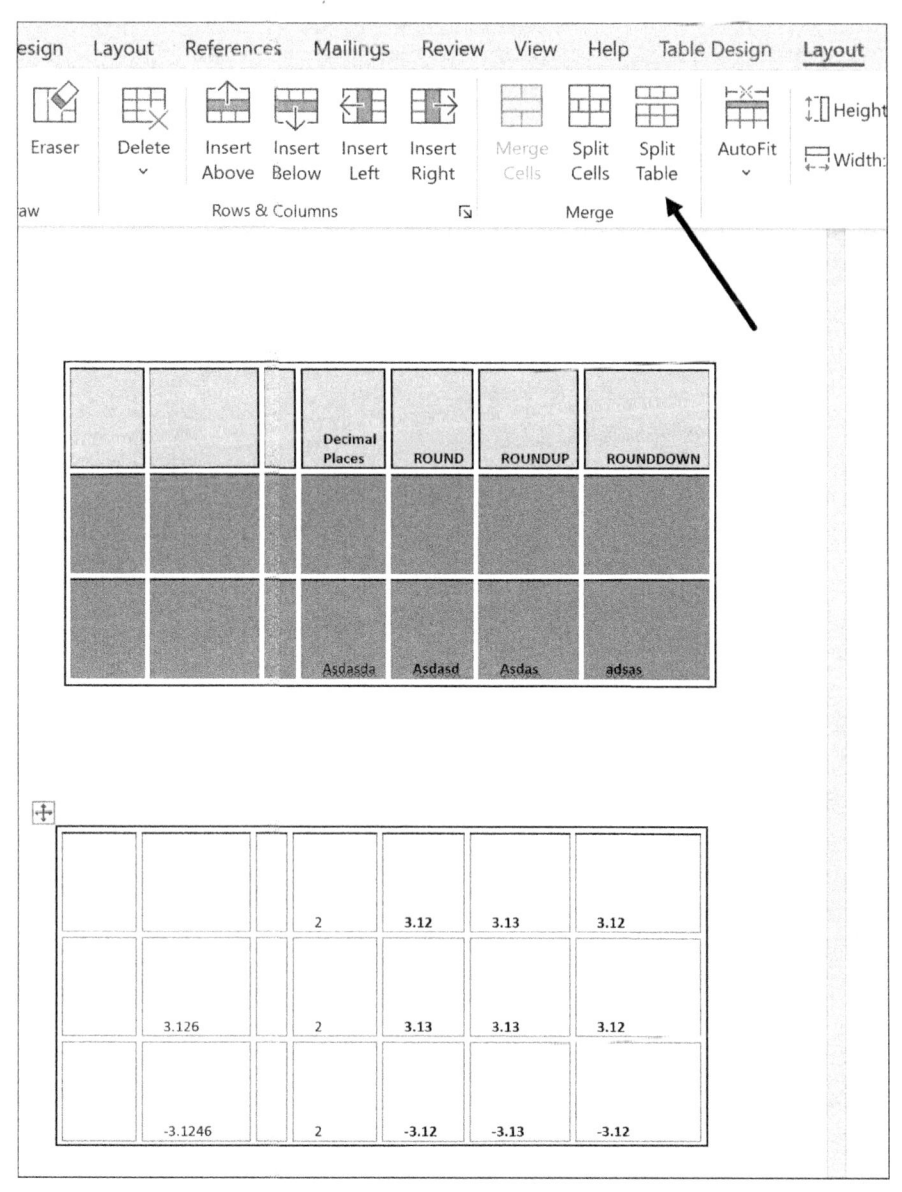

For whatever reason, when I just did this in my own document, it did split the tables but it placed them on top of one another, so I had to move one of the tables down to see both of them. (I don't recall it doing this in the past so I may have done something funky to cause that, but in case you do the same, that's how to fix it.)

Split Cells

You can split a cell in a table into multiple cells using the Split Cells option in the Merge section of the table Layout tab. Clicking on that option opens the Split Cells dialogue box which will let you specify a number of columns and rows for your split.

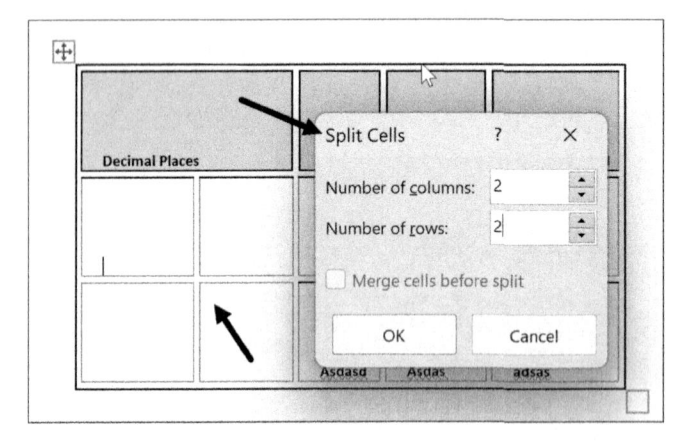

I believe I have used this before when I wanted to have a label row that covered more than one column, like Decimal Places now does above those two columns. But I may have also used Merge Cells for that instead.

This one is weird if there is already text in those cells. If you choose Merge Cells Before Split, it seems to bring that text up to the first X entries where X is the number of original cells in your selection. Otherwise, it puts the text in the left-most cell and doesn't let you split cells across rows. Best to do this before there's text involved.

Also, when you fill in the Split Cells dialogue box, the number of rows is the total number of rows for your selection, so if you selected two rows' worth of cells but then put 1 for the Number of Rows, that would actually merge those cells.

Merge Cells

To merge cells in a table, select the cells you want to merge and then use the Merge Cells option in the Merge section of the table Layout tab. It will automatically merge all of those cells and combine their contents into multiple rows of text within the cell.

Table Styles and Table Style Options

Finally, the Table Design tab has a number of Table Styles that are pre-formatted table style options:

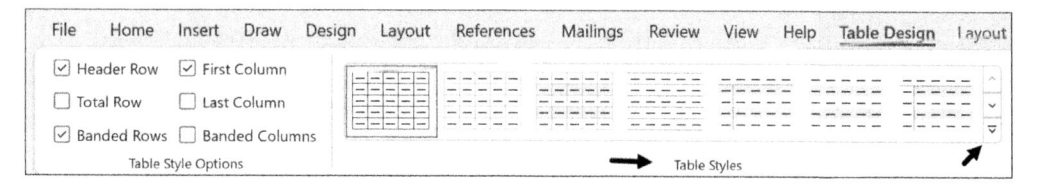

Click on the downpointing arrow with a line above it to see all of them:

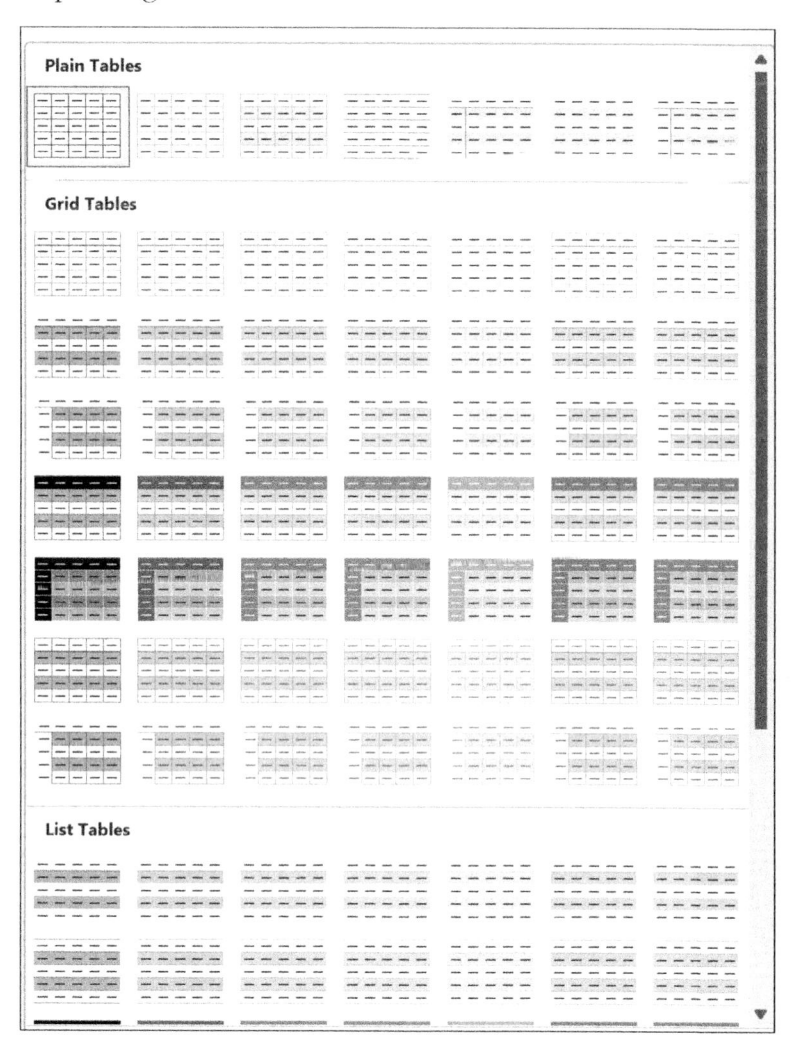

You'll have to use your scroll bar on the right-hand side to see the last few.

Click on any of those styles to apply it to your table. If you don't want to use the header row, first column, total row, last column, banded rows, or banded columns portion of the style, you can uncheck the box for that option in the Table Style Options section.

Or if you want to add that type of formatting, you can check those boxes.

As you check and uncheck those boxes the table styles will update to reflect how those changes will impact your table format. If the style has already been applied to your table, the table will also update.

I personally don't use table styles because they're never what I want so I just stick to a plain table style and then add my own shading as needed, but this is a way to get banded rows which can sometimes be useful. Just choose the Plain Table 1 option and uncheck Banded Columns if it's checked.

Appendix A: Basic Terminology Recap

These terms were covered in detail in *Word 365 for Beginners*. This is just meant as a refresher.

Tab

When I refer to a tab, I am referring to the menu options at the top of the screen. The tab options that are available by default are File, Home, Insert, Draw, Design, Layout, References, Mailings, Review, View, and Help, but for certain tasks additional tabs will appear.

Click

If I tell you to click on something, that means to move your cursor over to that location and then either right-click or left-click. If I don't say which to do, left-click.

Left-Click / Right-Click

A left-click is generally for selecting something and involves using the left-hand side of your mouse or bottom left-hand corner of your trackpad. A right-click is generally for opening a dropdown menu and involves using the right-hand side of your mouse or bottom right-hand corner of your trackpad.

Left-Click and Drag

Left-click and drag means to left-click and then hold that left-click as you move your mouse.

Dropdown Menu

A dropdown menu is a list of choices that you can view by right-clicking in a specific spot or clicking on an arrow next to or below one of the available choices under the tabs up top. Depending on where you are in the workspace, a dropdown menu may actually drop upward from that spot.

Expansion Arrow

In the bottom right corner of some of the sections under the tabs in the top menu you will see an arrow, which I refer to as an expansion arrow. Clicking on an expansion arrow will usually open a dialogue box or task pane and is often the way to see the largest number of options.

Dialogue Box

A dialogue box is a pop-up box that will open on top of your workspace and will usually include the largest number of choices for that particular setting or task.

Scroll Bar

Scroll bars appear when there are more options than can appear on the screen or when your document is longer than will show on the screen. They can be used to move through the remainder of the choices or document.

Task Pane

A task pane is a set of additional options that will appear to the sides or even below the main workspace. The Navigation pane is by default visible on the left-hand side of the workspace. You can close a task pane by clicking on the X in the top right corner of the pane.

Control Shortcuts

Control shortcuts are shortcuts that let you perform certain tasks in Word. I will write them as Ctrl + and then a character. That means to hold down both the Ctrl key and that character. So Ctrl + C means hold down Ctrl and C, which will let you copy your selection. Even though I will write each shortcut using a capital letter it doesn't have to be the capitalized version to work.

About the Author

M.L. Humphrey is a former stockbroker with a degree in Economics from Stanford and an MBA from Wharton who has spent close to twenty years as a regulator and consultant in the financial services industry.

You can reach M.L. at mlhumphreywriter@gmail.com or at mlhumphrey.com.

Printed in Great Britain
by Amazon